# How to

# BADMINTON

## a step·by·step guide

**Series editor:**
Mike Shaw

**Technical consultant:**
Clive Warren BA of E
Eastern Region Coach
for Coach Education

# JARROLD

Other sports covered in this series are:

| | |
|---|---|
| **AMERICAN FOOTBALL** | **SAILING A DINGHY** |
| **BASKETBALL** | **SNOOKER** |
| **BOWLS** | **SOCCER** |
| **COARSE FISHING** | **SQUASH** |
| **CRICKET** | **SWIMMING** |
| **CROQUET** | **TABLE TENNIS** |
| **GET FIT FOR SPORT** | **TENNIS** |
| **GOLF** | **WINDSURFING** |
| **HOCKEY** | |

How to play BADMINTON
ISBN 0-7117-0422-8

© Mike Shaw 1989
Illustrations by Malcolm Ryan

First published 1989
Reprinted 1992

Designed and produced by
Parke Sutton Limited, Norwich
for Jarrold Publishing, Norwich
Printed in Great Britain  2/92

# Contents

# Introduction

Badminton is an energetic indoor game that is especially enjoyable to play since, once the basics of the game are mastered, it also involves a good deal of tactical thought. It can be played by men and women of all ages, as doubles, mixed doubles or singles. Doubles is perhaps the more tactical game requiring good coordination between partners, whereas singles is more energetic and demands a higher level of fitness. In order to play either game you should be reasonably fit and in all cases ensure that you warm up properly before playing.

The basic equipment you will need is minimal and reasonably cheap to buy. To begin with you can either join a club or, more cheaply, hire one of the many badminton courts to be found in sports centres all around the country. Your local city council amenities department or library will give you a list of local courts, or you could contact the Badminton Association of England for more information. Courts are usually booked

for an hour and often need to be reserved well in advance. It is, of course, best to master the rudiments of the game by taking some lessons, though regular practice with a friend of a similar standard will also help to improve your game tremendously. Badminton is a game of touch and it may take a little time to acquire the necessary racket control, so practise as much as you can!

Once the basic strokes have been mastered, particularly the short and long service, the smash and the overhead clear, you may find that joining a club is the best answer for regular and varied play. Club play tends to revolve around the doubles and mixed doubles game and as such provides an excellent opportunity to find players of similar standards as well as good coaching, competitions and club evenings – and all the usual social facilities.

Badminton is an enjoyable game from the first time you set foot on the court, and once the subtleties of stroke play and the complexities of tactical play have been mastered, you will find the game even more of a delight to play.

# The Court

Badminton is played on an indoor court. It is a fast game, ideally played on wood, but other surfaces such as ashphalt are acceptable, providing they are level and not slippery.

Easy sighting of the shuttle is essential, therefore the lighting needs to be good and evenly spread over the court. Side lighting is best. The floor and surrounding walls should ideally be of a non-reflective dark colour. It is very difficult to play if there are windows in the court, as the shuttle's path becomes difficult to follow as it passes through different intensities of light.

The higher the ceiling the better – 30 feet is ideal, 25 feet is the minimum.

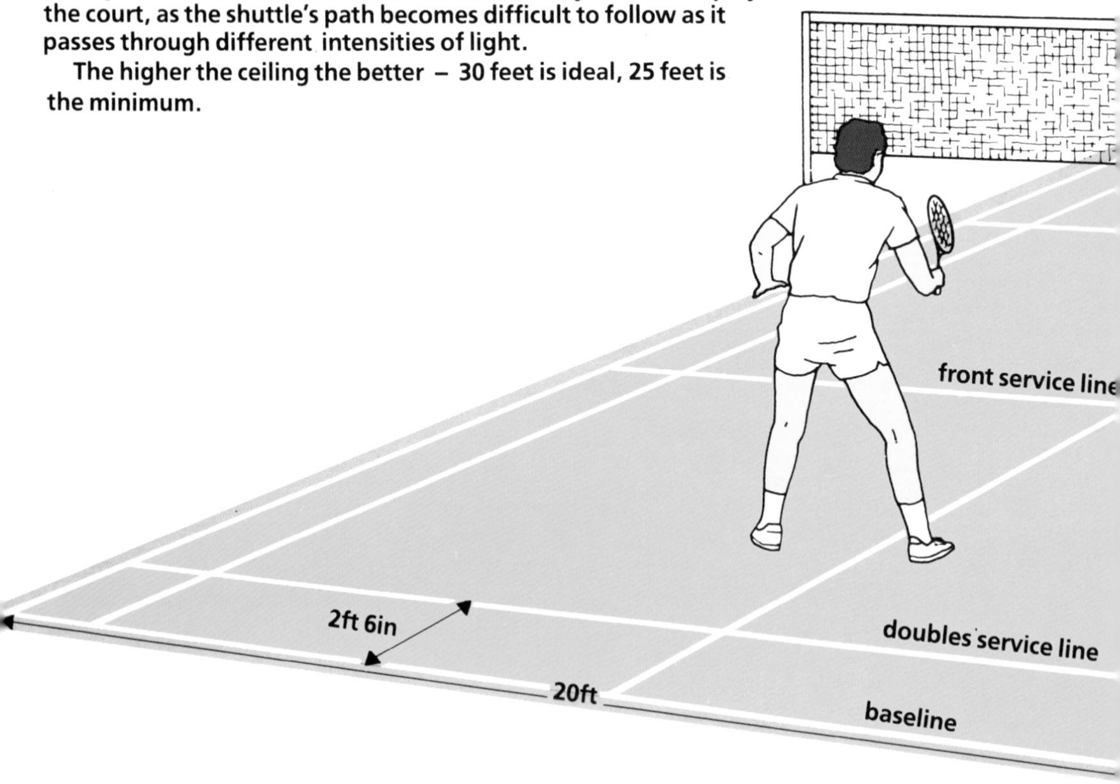

front service line

2ft 6in

20ft

doubles service line

baseline

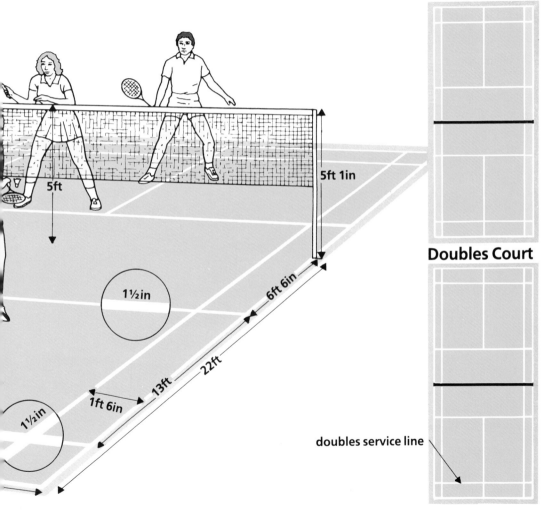

## Singles Court

## Doubles Court

5ft 1in

5ft

1½ in

6ft 6in

1½ in

1ft 6in

13ft

22ft

doubles service line

# Equipment

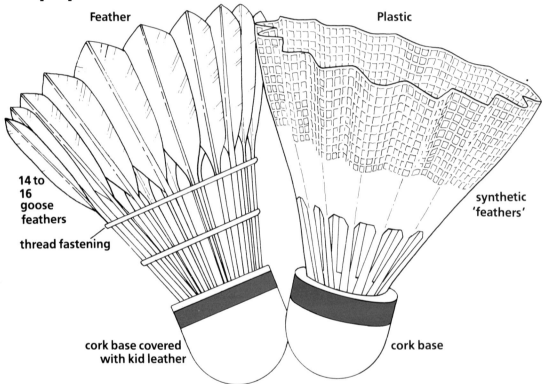

Feather

Plastic

14 to 16 goose feathers

thread fastening

synthetic 'feathers'

cork base covered with kid leather

cork base

## Shuttlecocks

Shuttlecocks or shuttles weigh about $\frac{1}{5}$th of an ounce. Speeds will vary according to conditions, a shuttle will fly further on clear day than a misty one for example. Ideally, if a player of average strength stands at one end of the court and plays an underarm stroke with a dropped shuttle, it should land between one foot and two foot six inches short of the same line at the other end of the court.

There are two types of shuttle. Feather ones, which are easily damaged and expensive, are the best to play with, and plastic, which are more durable (although you can expect to use two, or maybe three in the course of a match), less expensive, and perfectly acceptable for all but the best players.

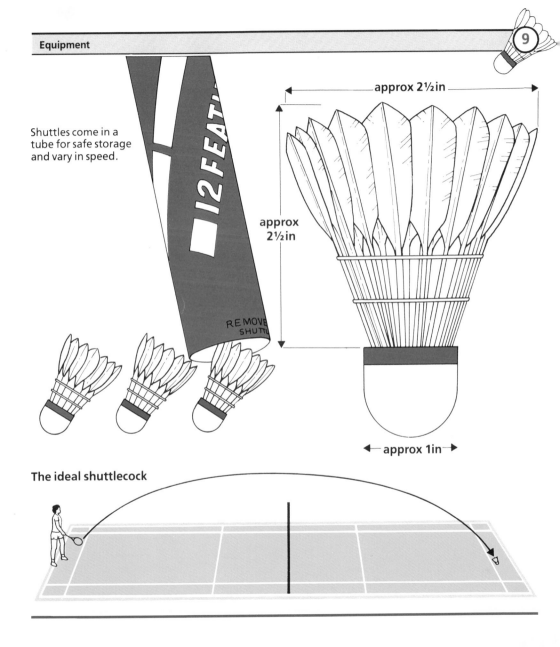

Shuttles come in a tube for safe storage and vary in speed.

approx 2½in

approx 2½in

12 FEAT

REMOVE SHUTT

approx 1in

**The ideal shuttlecock**

## Rackets

The racket is very light and tightly strung, weighing as little as 4 ounces, and consequently may be easily damaged. There are many types of rackets available today ranging from one-piece graphite, which is usually the most expensive, to graphite composite or aluminium head with steel shaft, to the cheapest all-steel variety. Ask a coach or sports shop for advice!

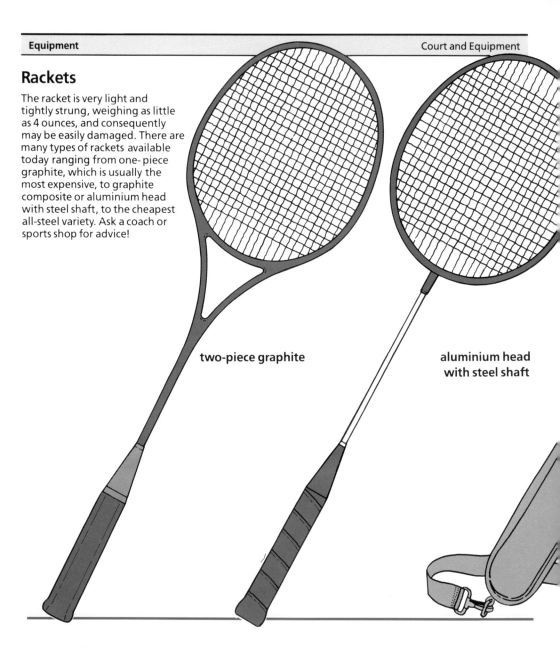

**two-piece graphite**

**aluminium head
with steel shaft**

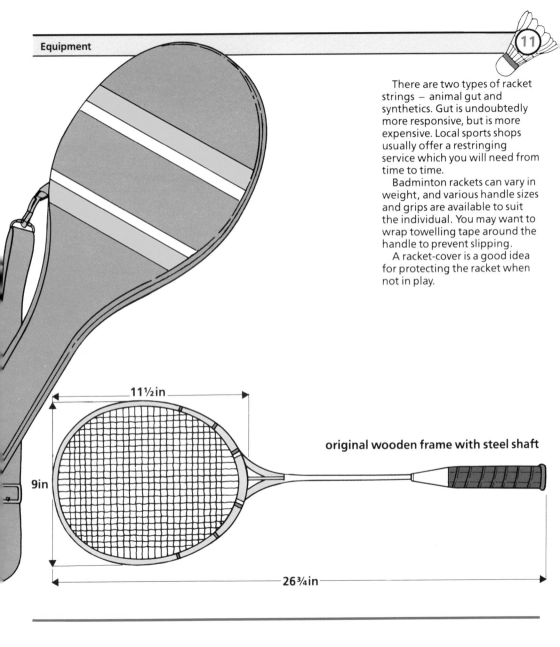

There are two types of racket strings – animal gut and synthetics. Gut is undoubtedly more responsive, but is more expensive. Local sports shops usually offer a restringing service which you will need from time to time.

Badminton rackets can vary in weight, and various handle sizes and grips are available to suit the individual. You may want to wrap towelling tape around the handle to prevent slipping.

A racket-cover is a good idea for protecting the racket when not in play.

11½in

9in

**original wooden frame with steel shaft**

26¾in

# Clothing

**Badminton involves stretching, turning and reacting quickly. Clothing therefore must primarily be unrestricting, allowing easy movement.**

A white shirt and shorts, skirt or dress are traditional though not necessary for informal games. A sweater and a tracksuit for warming-up are sensible additions.

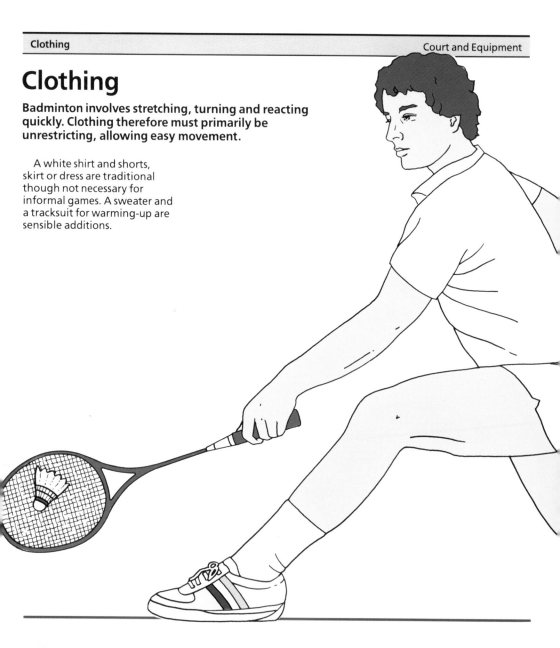

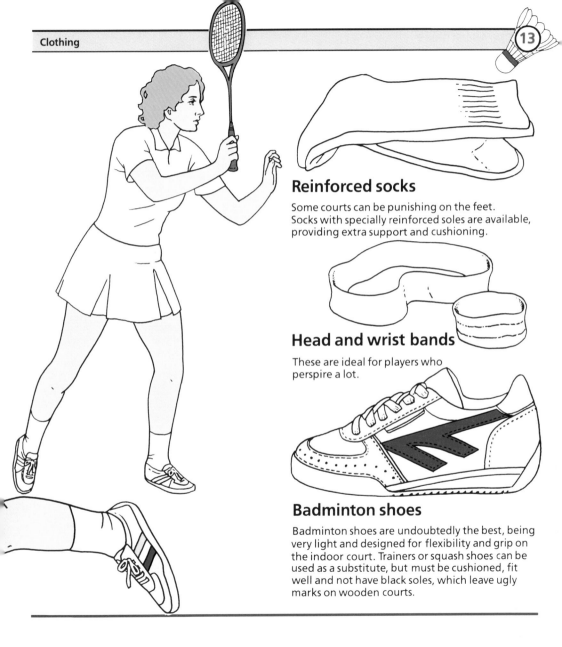

## Reinforced socks

Some courts can be punishing on the feet. Socks with specially reinforced soles are available, providing extra support and cushioning.

## Head and wrist bands

These are ideal for players who perspire a lot.

## Badminton shoes

Badminton shoes are undoubtedly the best, being very light and designed for flexibility and grip on the indoor court. Trainers or squash shoes can be used as a substitute, but must be cushioned, fit well and not have black soles, which leave ugly marks on wooden courts.

# Serving

## A correct service

**1** The server must have both feet inside the service area and on the ground at the moment of striking the shuttle.

**2** The shuttle must be dropped or thrown into the air with one hand and struck by the racket held with the other.

**3** The racket must strike the base or cork of the shuttle.

**4** The shuttle must be lower than the server's waist at the moment of impact.

**5** The head of the server's racket must be discernably lower than the hand at the moment of impact.

## Line calls

out

in in

in in

out

The shuttle must land in the receiving area. A shuttle on the line is in. The diagrams above and right illustrate line calls for serving in singles.

NOTE! It is the point of impact that counts not the final position of the shuttle.

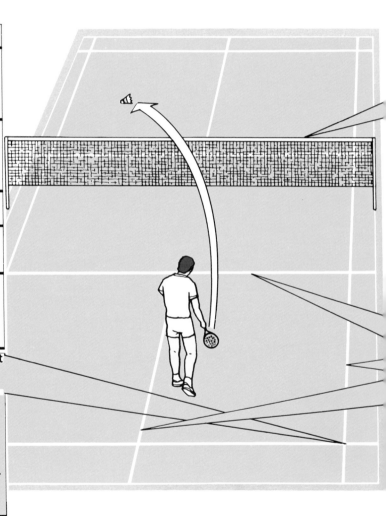

## Hitting the net

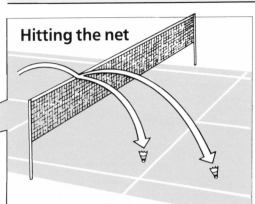

There is no such thing as a net call in badminton. Hitting the net is of no consequence. If the shuttle goes in it is a good service. If it goes out it is a fault.

## Foot faults

fault

fault

fault

At the moment of serving (when the racket hits the shuttle) the server (and the receiver) must have both feet on the ground within the service area. A foot on the line is a fault. The diagram above, for example, shows foot faults in the singles court.

# A Point

## The server gains a point if:

**1**

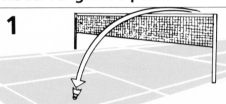

The shuttle lands within the playing area of the receiver's court.

**2**

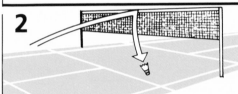

The receiver fails to return the shuttle.

**3**

The receiver returns the shuttle but it does not land in the playing area of the server's court.

# Scoring

After a service the shuttle must be returned using any part of the racket hitting any part of the shuttle to land within the playing area of the opponent's court before it touches the ground.

The players return the shuttle in this manner alternately until a rally ends.

### A rally ends if

**1** The shuttle hits the ground.

**2** The shuttle goes out of court.

**3** Another fault is made. (*see* pages 21 – 22)

### At the end of a rally

| If the server loses | If the receiver loses |
|---|---|
| Change of server. (*see* page 18) No change in score. | The server wins a point. No change in server. |

## A game

The first server (or pair) to win 15 points (11 points in ladies' singles) wins the game – unless set is called.

## A match

A match is usually the best of three games. If only one game is played it may, if wished, be played to 21 points.

## Setting

If a player or player(s) are within two points of winning a game (13 – 8 for example) and lose the serve and the opponents catch up (so the score is 13 – 13) then the player(s) who reached 13 first have the right to 'set'. (*see* table for exact details)

Once set is called the server continues to serve, but the score becomes 0 – 0 and so the service commences in the right-hand side of the court. The first player or players to win five points wins.

Set can also be called under the same circumstances one point from the end of a game, even if set was not called at two points (should the possibility have arisen). In this case the first player to three points wins. (*see* table for exact details)

| LADIES' SINGLES | FIRST TO |
|---|---|
| Set called at 9 – 9 | 3 |
| Set called at 10 – 10 | 2 |

| MENS' SINGLES | FIRST TO |
|---|---|
| Set called at 13 – 13 | 5 |
| Set called at 14 – 14 | 3 |

| DOUBLES | FIRST TO |
|---|---|
| Set called at 13 – 13 | 5 |
| Set called at 14 – 14 | 3 |

| GAMES TO 21 POINTS | FIRST TO |
|---|---|
| Set called at 19 – 19 | 5 |
| Set called at 20 – 20 | 3 |

## Changing ends

Players change ends after the first game (with the winner of the first game serving first).

Players also change halfway through the third game which varies according to the number of points being played.

| GAME | CHANGE ENDS AT |
|---|---|
| 11 points | First to 6 |
| 15 points | First to 8 |
| 21 points | First to 11 |

This equalizes the advantages or disadvantages of playing the different ends of the court.

# Serving and Receiving Courts

**Before starting to play a game, it is important to understand the differences between the singles and doubles courts for serving and rallies.**

## Singles

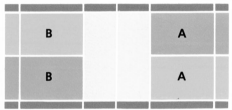

In singles the blue areas of the court are not used at all.

When serving from the right-hand side both server and receiver must be in their respective orange area. The shuttle is delivered from one orange area to land in the other. When serving from the left-hand side the same is true for the yellow areas.

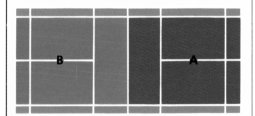

During the rally, when A returns to B, however, the shuttle can land anywhere in the red area. And when B returns to A it can land anywhere in the purple area.

## Doubles

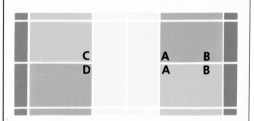

In doubles the blue areas of the court are used except during the service.

When serving from the right-hand side both server and receiver must be in their respective orange areas. The shuttle is delivered from one orange area to land in the other. When serving from the left-hand side the same is true for the yellow areas.

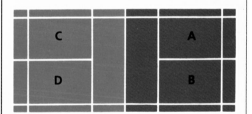

When A or B returns to C and D, however, the shuttle can land anywhere in the red area. And when C or D returns to A and B it can land anywhere in the purple area.

# The Toss

The game starts with the toss of a coin or racket to see who serves first and who starts at which end. The winner of the toss may decide either who starts serving or which end to play, but not both. The loser of the toss takes the decision that is left.

**If you win the toss you can either:**

| | | |
|---|---|---|
| **1** | Choose who serves first. | Your opponent chooses ends. |
| **2** | Choose ends. | Your opponent chooses who serves first. |

# Order of Serving

## Singles

1 Only the player serving can score a point in badminton but if the server loses a rally the service passes to the other player.
2 The first is always taken from the right-hand court.
3 After that, the service court used depends entirely upon the score of the server.
4 The winner of a game serves first in the next game.

| Right Service Court | Left Service Court |
|---|---|
| Server's score: 0 or any even number. | Server's score: any odd number. |

## Doubles

1 Only the team serving can score a point.
2 The partners in a team are considered as if they were one player. So, when the first player loses serve, it passes to the first player's partner instead of passing to the opposite team. Only when both players in a team have lost does the service pass to the opposite team.
   NOTE! The exception to this rule is the first service of a game which, when lost, passes directly to the opposite team.
3 Partners do not change sides when receiving. Both the serving and receiving teams decide at the beginning of each game which player will start on the right and which on the left. Only when a team scores a point do the partners exchange positions.
4 After a team's service is over the partners remain in their last serving positions to receive.
5 A team always starts to serve from the right-hand court with whichever partner is playing there.
6 The partner who is not serving or receiving may of course actually stand where they wish on their side of the net, providing they do not unsight the server or receiver.
7 The team which wins the game serves first in the next game. (see page 19 for an example of the doubles game)

# An Example of the Doubles Game

The complexities of scoring in doubles (*see* page 18) can perhaps best be explained by an example of the first few points of a game.

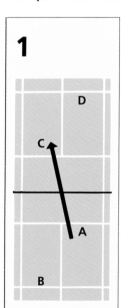

**1**

The game starts as usual in the right-hand side of the court.

A elects to serve first, C to receive first. A serves, C returns, there is a rally and eventually A&B win the point.

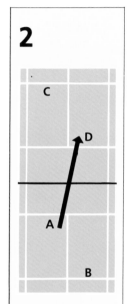

**2**

Score 1 – 0. As A&B won the point they retain the serve. A serves from the left to D. A&B lose the service and so remain with A on the left and B on the right. The service passes to C&D.

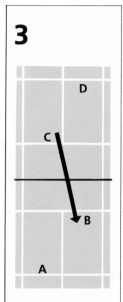

**3**

C&D to serve. Score 0 – 1. The first service of a turn is always played from the right-hand side. As C was receiving on the right C serves. B receives on the right. C loses the service and it passes to partner D.

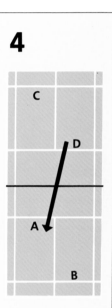

**4**

Score still 0 – 1. C&D have not scored so they do not change sides and D serves to A from the left.

# Service Faults

Any of the following service faults result in the server losing the service.

## 1 Mishitting the shuttle during service

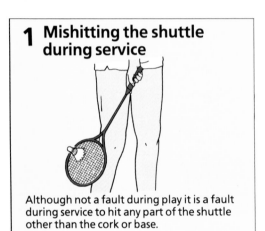

Although not a fault during play it is a fault during service to hit any part of the shuttle other than the cork or base.

## 2 Serving above the waist

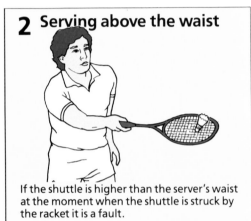

If the shuttle is higher than the server's waist at the moment when the shuttle is struck by the racket it is a fault.

## 3 Serving with a raised racket

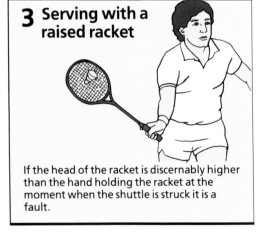

If the head of the racket is discernably higher than the hand holding the racket at the moment when the shuttle is struck it is a fault.

## 4 Foot faults during service

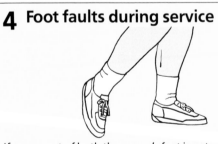

If some part of both the server's feet is not stationary on the ground and inside the lines of the service area it is a fault. Equally if at the moment of service some part of both the receiver's feet is not inside the receiving area and on the ground it is a fault.

## 5 Missing the shuttle

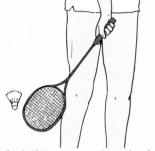

It is a fault if the server misses the shuttle altogether when serving.

## 6 Service feints

It is a fault if the server attempts to deceive the receiver during or before service. The service must be one continuous deliberate forward movement.

# General Faults

It is possible to lose a rally for infringements of the code of play. These are called faults.

## 1 Hitting obstructions

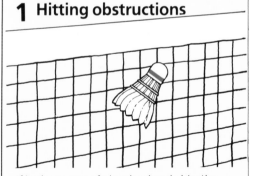

If in the course of play the shuttle hits the roof, or the lights, or goes through the net, it is a fault.

## 2 Sling shots and double hits

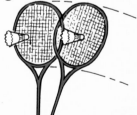

A sling shot, which is where a shuttle is caught momentarily on the racket and then thrown across the net, rather than struck cleanly, is a fault. Similarly if the shuttle is struck twice in succession by a player or if both players in doubles hit the shuttle in succession it is a fault.

## 3 Touching the net

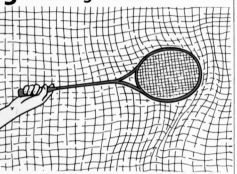

If the net or poles are touched during play by any means whatsoever – racket, body, sleeve etc. – then the offender loses the rally whatever the outcome of play.

## 4 Touching the shuttle

If the shuttle is touched (other than by the racket) or deflected, or lands on a player during play then the offender loses the rally even if contact with the shuttle was entirely accidental, or beyond the player's control.

## 5 Playing the shuttle in the opponent's court

Striking the shuttle before it comes over the net, in other words anticipating a return or service while it is still in the opponent's court, is a fault. It is not a fault, however, to allow the racket or arm to follow through over the net after a stroke providing the net is not touched.

## 6 Interfering with play

If an opponent's game is interfered with (deliberately or not) it is a fault. Examples would be sliding under the net into the opponent's court, losing control of the racket so that it flies into an opponent's court, or standing between the server and receiver in doubles so impairing the server's view of the court.

# Non Faults Some actions which appear to be faults are, in fact, not.

## 1 Serving when the opponent isn't ready

If the server serves and the receiver is not ready and makes no attempt to return the shuttle then the server is obliged to serve again. If any attempt is made to return the shuttle, however, the receiver is deemed to have been ready.

## 2 Playing round the post

If during a rally the player, perhaps uncertain that a shot is out, plays it back for safety, and instead of going over the net it passes round the outside of the pole and lands in a valid part of the opponent's court, it is (somewhat suprisingly) a valid return.

## 3 Serving from the wrong court

If the server serves from the wrong court and wins the rally but this is discovered before the next service is delivered, the serve may be taken again from the correct court.

## 4 Receiving in the wrong court

If in doubles the receivers are standing on the wrong sides and win the rally the server may opt to play the point again provided this is discovered before the next service.

## 5 Interference to play

If there is interference from another court, or the shuttle sticks in the net having passed over it the point is played again. A player falling over, or suffering from a broken racket, or losing a shoe, however, must take the consequences. If the shuttle breaks play continues.

# The Grip

It is most important that the badminton racket is held with the correct grip. There are two main grips, one for the forehand and one for the backhand. Using these correctly will help greatly to improve stroke play.

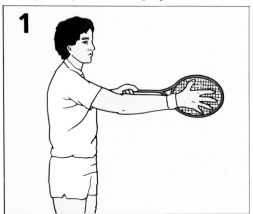

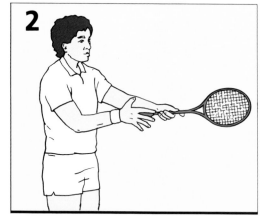

## How to find the forehand grip

1. Hold out the racket in front of you with the head vertical.
2. Slide your right hand (if you are right-handed) from the strings to the handle.
3. Shake hands with the handle. The end of the handle should be just below the ball of your thumb.

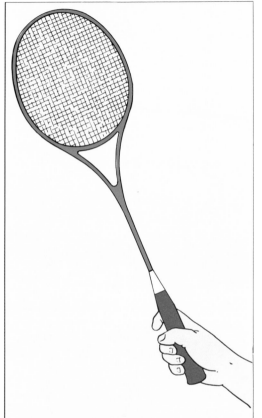

## The forehand grip

The forefinger often provides the lever in the forehand stroke. The difference between forehand and backhand is a rotation of about 30°. The changeover will come naturally once you start to play certain shots and you will have the grip to play them more effectively.

## The backhand grip

This is slightly different to the forehand grip. The thumb is along the flat back of the handle to pass on the snap of the wrist to the racket.

# The Short Service

Serving is always performed diagonally across the court. There are several variations, however, and learning to master these will strengthen your game considerably.

The short service is usually aimed towards the centre line to reduce angles of reply. Serving to the outside edges of the opponent's service area invites passing returns down the outside but can be advantageous in reducing the opponent's ability to attack the serve.

**Forehand**

**Short serve trajectory**

## Backhand

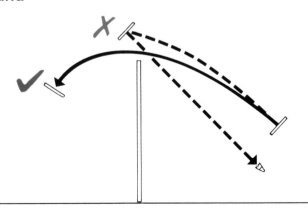

Keep the trajectory of the short service down. If it is a few inches above the net, the opponent will pounce and smash the shuttle downwards. With practice, this shot can 'graze' the net and drop virtually on the intersection of the centre and service lines.

# The Long Service

This serve is generally not used against experienced players in doubles who will smash the return. In singles the long service forces the receiver to the back of the court and can be useful for varying the game. In mixed doubles, the long service may be used when the woman is receiving service since she will be outmanoeuvred to the rearcourt and the positions of the man and woman will thus be reversed. (*see* pages 44 – 45)

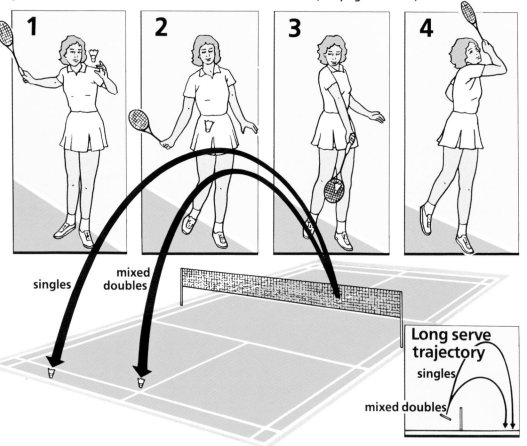

**1**

**2**

**3**

**4**

singles

mixed doubles

Long serve trajectory

singles

mixed doubles

# Flick and Drive Serves

These are deceptive shots using the short service stance and delivery (forehand or backhand). Feigning a short service, at the last minute the shot is flicked or hit hard over the player's head, causing a poor shot or mishit return.

Very effective when played to the backhand, these serves provide excellent variation to keep receivers guessing.

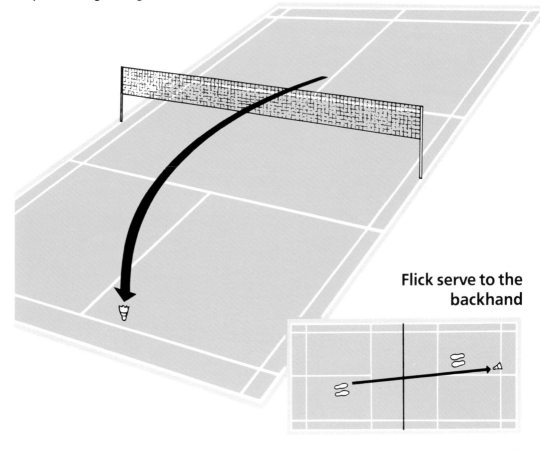

**Flick serve to the backhand**

# Return of Service

Very good players are so fast they can stand close to the service line confident that they can move in time to return any type of serve.

They punish any short serve that is too high with a 'kill shot' – a vicious tap of the racket which sends the shuttle directly and almost unplayably to the floor; and they will attack low short serves the moment they are over the net with tap shots or pushes to the farthest corners of the court.

Beginners, however, have to allow for their deficiencies. Drive and flick serves will catch you flat-footed, hopefully waving your racket as the shuttle passes by. Long serves will leave you miles out of position struggling to get back for a drop shot just returned over the net. You will also find very high serves hard to judge as they finish their trajectory practically spent, falling vertically.

The answer is a compromise. Adopt an alert stance on the balls of your feet ready to go forward or back with the racket poised. Stand a yard or so back from the front service line. You will lose speed at the net, but find you have a little longer to move forward for flicks and drives and back for long serves.

# Effective Replies

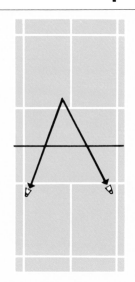

## Flick and drive service reply

Attack whenever possible with a well-placed smash, or a fast drop may be possible in doubles. Play smashes (with a good safety margin) to the sidelines or try one direct to the body of your opponent. This will often be rewarded with a defensive shot from the body which can usually be killed.

If you are not fast enough to get a smash in, then drive or clear to the rear court.

## Long service reply

Smashing effectively from the back of the court requires quite a lot of technique. You must get there before the shuttle, get behind it and return quickly to the best position to cover the reply.

Beginners, however, are probably safer attempting an overhead clear as a return, which will force your opponent(s) to the rearcourt. It is important to get good height and depth – if the shuttle is hit short you make it too easy for your opponent to step back and hit the shuttle downwards; if your clear is too low it may be intercepted midcourt.

The purpose is to go over the top of your opponents, making them run to the back of the court and wait for the shuttle, giving you time to get back in position.

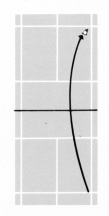

## Short service reply

Obviously you kill everything you can, otherwise play shots as close to the net as you dare or push to the far corners. In doubles, it is advantageous to play *between* the players down the centre.

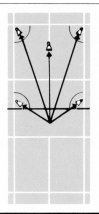

# Positioning During Rallies

Before demonstrating the basic strokes it is important to understand that you are defending your court and attacking your opponent's.

## Singles

Your position wants to be astride the centre line and forward of half way. How far forward will depend on your speed, but remember the shuttle decelerates rapidly and takes longer to get to the back of the court than the front.

## Doubles

The location of base position in doubles is more complex, depending on whether the team is attacking or defending, and may change during the course of a rally (*see* page 42).

Remember that you are trying to get the shuttle onto your opponent's floor, so any shot you hit upwards is defensive. Adopt an alert stance up on the balls of your feet. Remember you may have to go left or right, forward or back. Hold the racket in front of you ready to deal with shots to the body. Wait with your racket at head height if you have hit the shuttle down, waist height if you have hit the shuttle up.

Once you are at base, alert and perfectly balanced, you are in a good position. By keeping one foot where it is and lungeing forward, left or right, with your arm extended, you can cover a surprisingly large area. You should have time to move back for any shots placed behind you.

In singles, after every stroke aim to get back to your centre spot as fast as possible. If your opponent forces you badly out of position then buy time with a high shot or a lob. Beginners often pause to admire their own shots. Remember hitting the shuttle is only the first part of a stroke; getting back on position is the second.

## Base position for singles

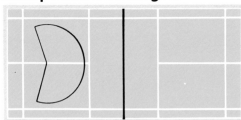

## The lunge

> **Remember: watch as your opponent hits the shuttle as this may tell you what is going to be done with it. Then watch the shuttle very closely as it is returned.**

# The Smash

This is the ultimate attacking shot to play when you can get behind the shuttle.

Watch the shuttle carefully — never take your eyes off it for a second. Then attack the shuttle while it is in front of you by throwing the racket head at it in a downward direction, and follow through with the racket arm.

Imagine you are throwing a ball as hard as you can. You would draw back your arm and hurl the ball, giving it that final flick with your wrist to send it on its way. Do that with the racket. The steeper the trajectory the better. This stroke needs practice but is well worth perfecting.

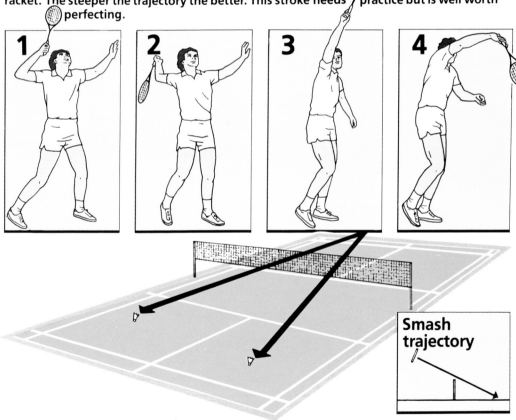

**1** **2** **3** **4**

Smash
trajectory

# Returning the Smash

A good smash will be very fast and very steep. It will be aimed either well away from you, or straight at you.

Position and alertness are very important. Watch your opponent's racket and the shuttle. The sooner you get a 'fix' on the path of the shuttle the more chance you have. Never for a second stop watching the shuttle after it has been hit.

As a beginner your choices are limited. At first you will be glad to even get to the shuttle. Frequently you will stick your racket in the way and mishit the shuttle or make an easy hit for your opponent.

As you get better try to anticipate well enough to drive the return – either to some difficult corner or maybe straight at the opponent.

In singles try the block shot. Take all the sting out of the smash by playing with a firm racket grip but meet the shuttle with little movement of the racket. With practice, the shuttle should return just over the net.

# The Overhead Clear

This is normally a defensive shot, useful when you can't get sufficiently behind the shuttle to play an attacking shot. The shuttle has normally been hit high and is falling at the back of the court. Step backwards to get yourself *under* the shuttle (so it would land on your back foot) and play the same approach as the smash, but then hit the shuttle when it is directly above you and send it high over the net to the back of your opponent's court. Try to get it within an inch or so of the baseline. Remember you are out of position at the moment you hit the shuttle, so hit it high enough to give yourself time to get back into position.

To play the shot backhand – turn and follow the shuttle and position yourself under it (so it would land on your front foot) and play the shot with your back to the net. The racket head should be aimed at the shuttle with explosive acceleration. This shot needs practice.

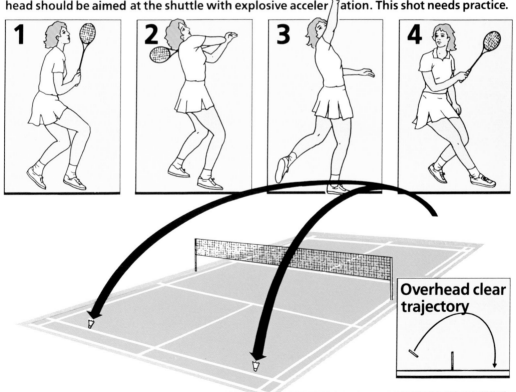

**Overhead clear trajectory**

# The Drive

The drive is an excellent attacking answer to a wide return from your opponent and is usually played when the opponent's shot is waist-height and of poor length. This shot is hit hard with a flat-faced racket to pass low and flat over the net, either cross-court or down the line, hopefully bypassing your opponent in the process.

The rear foot stays pretty well in the centre position, with all the weight on the other leg for the shot; the player then pushes off the front leg and back to upright and into position.

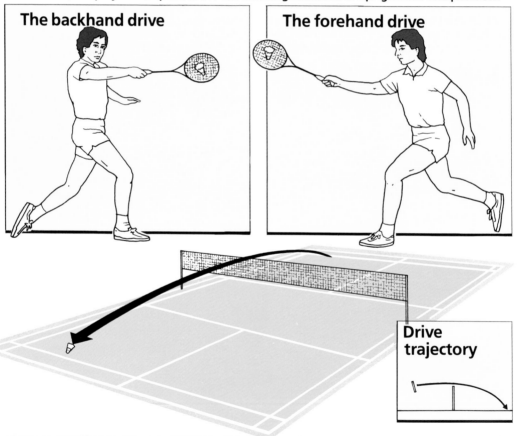

The backhand drive

The forehand drive

Drive trajectory

# The Lob

The lob is used to lift the shuttle from the forecourt or midcourt high over the net, forcing your opponent to the rearcourt. It can be played forehand or backhand and is more commonly used in singles than doubles.

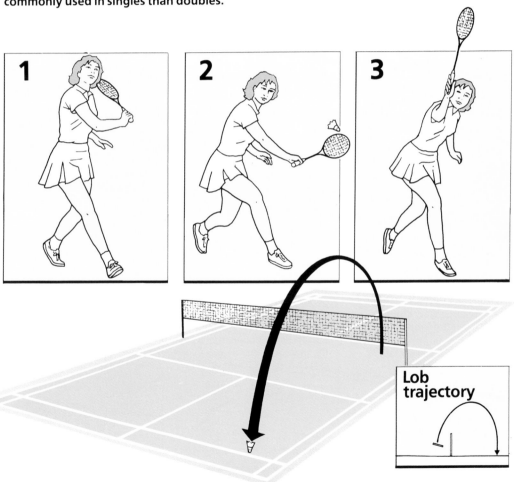

**Lob trajectory**

# Disguised Shots

Disguised shots can be extremely useful in turning a rally to your advantage since your opponent will be caught off guard and probably produce a weak return shot. Approach the hitting point with the preparation and stance for the expected shot so that your opponent misreads your intentions, then change tactics at the last moment.

## Disguised drop

A very effective shot. Make as if to smash then hold back to hit the shuttle downward and without power so it falls just over the net.

## Disguised attack clear

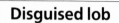

The shuttle should be hit powerfully with a flattish trajectory but out of your opponent's reach. The idea is to force your opponent to the rearcourt to play an unbalanced return shot.

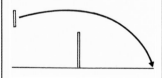

## Disguised lob

Very satisfying shot if your opponent is already in at the net anticipating your net shot. Hold the hand cocked back until the last split second then bring the hand through using the wrist to flick the shuttle over your opponent's head.

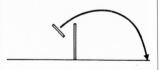

# Net Shots

Net shots vary from featherlight upward touch shots to downward 'kill' strokes and they must all be played very close to the net to be effective.

## Cross-court net

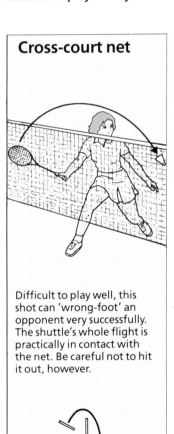

Difficult to play well, this shot can 'wrong-foot' an opponent very successfully. The shuttle's whole flight is practically in contact with the net. Be careful not to hit it out, however.

## Kill off the net

Move quickly to the net and tap the shuttle downwards to 'kill' it.

## Net shot

This shot is played to make the opponent lift the shuttle. If you are too late to hit the shuttle above the net for a 'kill', let the shuttle drop and play it near to the tape, hitting it softly just over the net so that it drops close to the net.

# Positions and Tactics in Singles

## Serving and receiving positions

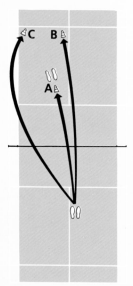

The server nearly always stands close to the centre line. It is possible to serve from the outside line cross-court into the back of the receiving court but this leaves the server out of position. Serves are short to A, flick to B and lob to C. Beware of serving to the middle or outside front of the receiving area since you will invite drives down outside line.

The receiver adopts a position almost in the centre of the receiving court to cover all possibilities.

## Base position

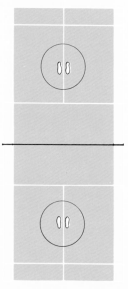

Once the rally is underway players should seek to maintain base position. This strong central area enables the player rapidly to cover front, back and sides with the minimum of movement.

## Drawing the opponent away from base

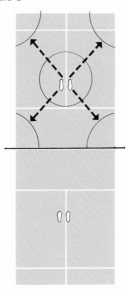

The object of every stroke, whether defensive or attacking, should be to place the shuttle in a position that draws the opponent away from base. For example, use an overhead clear to the backhand corner to create time for yourself to get back to base.

## Playing into space

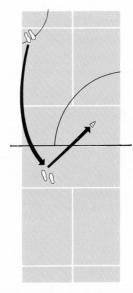

Once an opponent has been drawn away from base aim to play your next shot into the space you have created. Be aware of your opponent's momentum and use that to your advantage as well. A player moving back after a drop can be dropped again. A player moving forward to the net can be lobbed or passed with a drive down the side.

# Positions and Tactics in Doubles

## Serving and receiving positions

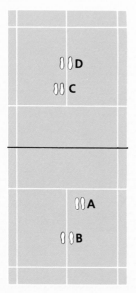

The server stands in the classic serving position (A) with the partner (B) in a commanding position further back. The receiver (C) stands forward as the serve in doubles is nearly always short – lob serves are likely to be smashed. The receiver's partner (D) adopts a similar central position to the server's partner.

## Basic attacking and defending formations

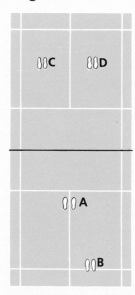

The attacking formation has one player forward (A), racket raised ready to pounce on poor returns, the other player (B) at the back ready to deal with overhead clears. In the defending position both players defend their half of the court (C,D).

Doubles players must learn to synchronise their movements. This can only be done by talking to each other both before and during play. The transition from attacking to defensive position and vice-versa should be smooth and reflexive.

# Wedge defence

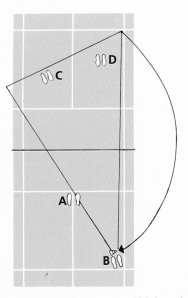

If, in defence, the shuttle is returned high and into a corner, the defending players (C, D) should then imagine a circle radiating from the shuttle and both move to be equidistant from it, forming a wedge shape.

The back player (B) has been drawn wide to play the shuttle and so the front player (A) takes up position in the forecourt as shown.

# Undefended areas

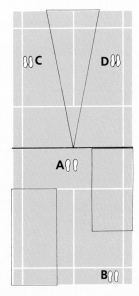

Players must always be aware of the areas they are leaving undefended. Players in a defensive position (C, D) that is too widely spread invite shots between them. Attacking players (A, B) playing too far forward or to the side can equally leave large areas undefended.

# Positions and Tactics in Mixed Doubles

In mixed doubles, the service to the man is often short and to the lady it is often high. In the short service to the man, the lady whose partner is serving always remains in the left-hand court close to the centre line, whether her partner is serving from the right or the left (*see* diagrams 1 and 2). In this position she does not obscure the server's view but remains forward ready to cover the net both left and right. After serving, the man should drop back to a base position to defend the court, much as in singles, with the lady poised at the net ready for the kill.

When the lady serves to the man, the service is still short but the players adopt the same positions as for serving in ordinary doubles play (*see* page 42).

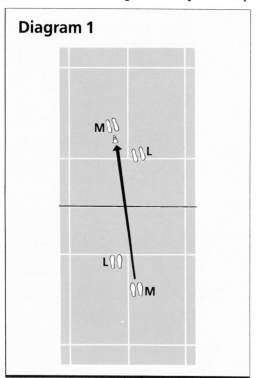

**Diagram 1**

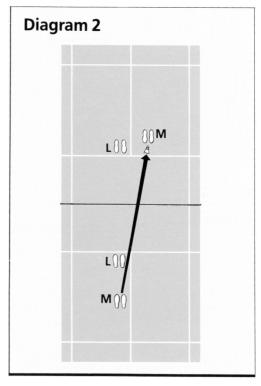

**Diagram 2**

A high serve to the lady could result in the lady being drawn to the back of the court while the man is forced to cover the net, so reversing the roles.

The lady's reply should therefore be to drop or smash to the areas shown; she then follows the shuttle in quickly to take up her position at the net while the man drops back to base (*see* diagram 3). However, should her intentions be read by the opponents, then she could instead clear cross-court to the back corner or try a cross-court drop to unsettle the opponents' momentum (*see* diagram 4).

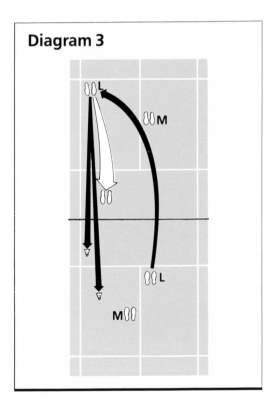

## Diagram 3

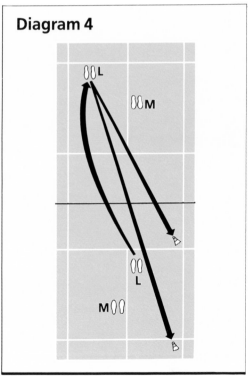

## Diagram 4

# Bad Habits

## Taking the shuttle too late

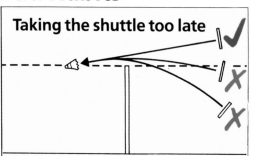

Many players develop the habit of playing the shuttle too late. Remember if you hit the shuttle below net height you are hitting upwards and therefore playing defensively. Only when you hit downwards are you really attacking.

## Bent elbow

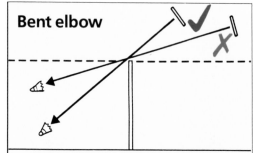

There is a tendency amongst players to play smashes with the elbow bent. Remember the net is five feet high – so you need every inch you can find to play effectively. Reach up for a smash, and take it as early as you can to get the angle of descent as steep as possible.

## The tight grip

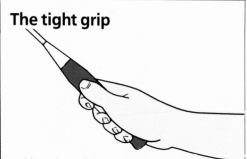

Holding the racket too tightly is not only very bad for you because the tensions in the forearm and elbow can produce tennis elbow, but also it will not help your stroke play. Imagine if the lightest grip you can have is 1 and the tightest white-knuckle grip is 10, then you should aim for 5 or 6.

## Head drop

It is noticeable, particularly when playing the lunge, that some players allow their head to drop forward. This is not a good idea since firstly the eyes are no longer watching the shuttle – which can be fatal – and secondly it affects balance and can lead to players toppling forward.

# Good Habits

## Courtesy on court

When playing badminton without an umpire – as most people do – players are dependent upon each other for line calls. It is essential, therefore, that you give your opponent the benefit of the doubt. Also, try not to get into the habit of blaming your partner in doubles, but think positively instead.

## Check equipment

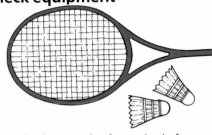

Always check your racket for tension before and after a game. The tension can go out of strings and your shots will lack speed as a result. Make sure too that you have some good shuttles. All of us have a tendency to collect tubes full of damaged ones.

## Warming up

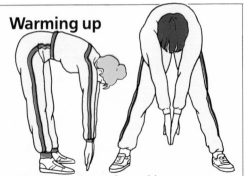

Badminton halls are often cold so wear a tracksuit and warm up with someone before playing. This will prevent strained muscles and improve your mobility in the early points. Don't forget to put your tracksuit on if you have to sit out between games.

## Check the conditions

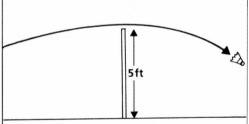

5 ft

Temperature and humidity greatly affect the flight of the shuttle. Always get on court and try a few shuttles for length before playing. Play a few high serves and ask your opponent to tell you where they land. It's also worth checking that the net is the correct height.

# Glossary

**BASELINE** The furthermost line from the net, marking the end of the court, except when serving in doubles. (*see* page 17)

**BASE POSITION** The central part of the court from which most areas of the court can be reached. Players should aim to return to this position as fast as possible after every shot.

**DOUBLES SERVICE LINE** The line in the rearcourt between the baseline and the front service line, marking the end of the doubles service court.

**DRIVE** A return taken above waist height and driven over the net almost horizontally, often down the sidelines.

**DRIVE SERVE** A hard service driven, often directly at the receiver, at chest or head height. Played for its variety only.

**DROP SHOT** A shot, usually tapped or pushed, played from the rearcourt, overhead and hit down to the forecourt or midcourt.

**FLICK** Any shot played predominantly with the wrist.

**FLICK SERVE** A serve played mostly with the wrist in which the shuttle is hit past the receiver's shoulder and lands near the rear service line.

**FRONT SERVICE LINE** The line closest to the net behind which the server and receiver must stand during service.

**KILL** A return taken close to the net, while the shuttle is still above the net, and hit sharply downwards.

**LET** A rally, the result of which is not scored. To 'play a let' means to play that point again.

**LOB** A shot used to lift the shuttle over an opponent, forcing them to the rearcourt.

**LONG SERVE** A long, high serve where the shuttle is hit high over the net to drop into the rearcourt.

**LUNGE** A shuttle taken at full stretch with the weight on the leading leg which is fully bent.

**NET SHOT** A delicate return in which the shuttle just tumbles over the net.

**OVERHEAD CLEAR** A shot played instead of a smash on a high but falling shuttle which is then sent high to the back of the opponent's court.

**POINT** A rally, the result of which is scored if won by the server. If won by the receiver, however, the service passes to the receiver with no change in score.

**PUSH** The shuttle is hit with a smooth, stroking action and follow through.

**RALLY** The period during which the shuttle is in play.

**SETTING** The procedure whereby if one player equals the other's score at one or two points from game, extra points may be played to decide the winner of the game if desired. (*see* page 18)

**SHORT SERVE** A low, short serve – the shuttle skims the net, landing just beyond the front service line.

**SLING SHOT** A shot where the shuttle is not struck cleanly off the racket but is instead slung forward by it. Usually acknowledged as a fault.

**SMASH** A shot used on a high shuttle in which the racket strikes the shuttle at its highest point as hard as possible and at a steep angle.

**TAP** The shuttle is hit with a short racket movement, using a tapping action.

# St Catherine's
## Chapel
## at Abbotsbury

## and the Legend
## of the Saint

*To* Martin B. Radcliffe
*a staunch supporter*
*and valued friend*
*of Abbotsbury Music*

Published by Abbotsbury Music,
9A West Street, Abbotsbury, Dorset DT3 4JT. Tel: 01305 871475
Registered charity 1056261
St Catherine's website: www.st-catherine.org.uk

First published 1999

A CIP catalogue record for this book is available from the British Library
ISBN: 0 9536402 0 5

Design: AL Art, Askerswell, Dorset, DT2 9EN
Print: Warwick Press, Weymouth, Dorset DT4 9TJ

# St Catherine's Chapel at Abbotsbury

LAURENCE KEEN

St Catherine's Chapel, on its hill above the village of Abbotsbury in west Dorset, forms a dramatic landmark and seamark. From a platform of level ground, its 'fearfully exposed position' (as Thomas Hardy described it) gives extensive views south-east across the Fleet to Portland, and west across Lyme Bay to Torbay in Devon. Below, in a protective fold in the hills, lie the village, and the ruins of the great monastery which built the rugged little chapel to St Catherine in the fourteenth century. St Catherine's Chapel remains the most poignant reminder of Abbotsbury's monastic past.

The early history of Abbotsbury Abbey and its monastic community is uncertain, although the place name 'Abbedesbury' (manor of the abbot), which appears in a document of the first half of the tenth century, must imply the presence of a community by that time. From the eleventh century, more information is available.

Orc (who was presumably Scandinavian), a nobleman serving in the household of King Cnut, married Tola (her name gives rise to the place name Tolpuddle). The king gave Orc the manor of Portesham in 1023, and soon after this Orc set up a guild or fraternity of St Peter at Abbotsbury. It is thought that Orc and Tola first established a house of secular canons, which was later re-formed as a Benedictine monastery with monks from Cerne Abbey. Certainly, Orc and Tola's estates passed eventually to the abbey and were the core holding of the abbey's estates at the time of the Domesday Book. Orc's bones, 'inclosed in a daintie Marbill coffin' which was eventually removed to the parish church in Abbotsbury, are said to have been seen there in the sixteenth century. The abbey was dissolved in 1539; gatehouses and other parts of the monastery survive, but the most impressive building to remain is the massive tithe barn which probably dates from about 1400.

St Catherine's Chapel was built in the fourteenth century at a time when the abbey was suffering from exposure to French invaders, with its coffers depleted by the cost of raising forces to defend the coast, and by bad financial management. It was no doubt intended, in its dramatic position on high ground above the village, as a symbol of abbatial authority.

Why St Catherine was chosen as the dedication saint is probably due to the chapel's hilltop location, and has parallels with other sites where chapels were dedicated to St Catherine. The situation also bears comparison with that of St Michael's Church on Glastonbury Tor, and of the parish church, also dedicated to St Michael, on Brent Tor in Devon. No archaeological excavations have taken place round St Catherine's Chapel at Abbotsbury, but excavations on Glastonbury Tor in 1964–66 revealed Saxon and medieval material underneath and around the surviving tower, which may in turn suggest an earlier use of the hilltop at Abbotsbury.

St Catherine's Chapel is no run-of-the-mill affair. In spite of its small size (internally it is 42 ft long and 14 ft wide), it is colossal in construction. Its rugged walls are some 4 ft thick and the entire building, roof and all, is constructed of stone. The solid stone roof is astonishing, as are the massive buttresses with a pierced arcaded parapet of three openings between them, and the tall octagonal stair turret in the north-west corner.

The turret gives access to the roof parapet, but is carried higher. Surprisingly, the narrow stone steps lead into a small chamber, lit on the south-west and north by narrow, square-headed slits, and on the east by what was originally a double-light window with foiled heads. From this largest window there is an uninterrupted view over the chapel roof to the monastery below. Immediately beneath the window, on the north side, is one of the supports

for a small altar, indicating that this small room was used as a chapel. Of additional interest is the flat ceiling divided originally into eight panels with trefoils on the outer edges. The ceiling is supported by an octagonal column with a large capital of two stones decorated with foliage; the upper one has eight shields, the lower one four; all are now indecipherable except one which has a chevron between three swans carved on it. Between the carved stones oyster shells are visible, used by the masons to level the stones of the capital.

Unusually, the chapel has both a north and south porch; both are vaulted in stone, as is the pointed tunnel vault of the chapel itself. Inside, the vault has eight transverse ribs, divided by further moulded ribs to make twenty-four panels. The panels on both the north and south sides culminate in five-foiled heads. The main bay divisions have decorated bosses with foliated carving, one animal carving, and one human. With its original painted decoration, the stone vault would have been indistinguishable from a conventional timber vault, and in terms of scale and acoustic would have rivalled any space in the abbey church. The surviving chapel fittings include brackets in the east wall, a piscina and a stone recess. There can be little doubt that a building of this quality would originally have had fine stained glass in its windows. Some of the original Perpendicular tracery remains.

It is hard to find parallels for these unusual design features. The nearest example of a similar stone vault and solid stone roof is at the twelfth-century St Aldhelm's Chapel at Worth Matravers in Dorset, and in

Somerset, the north chantry chapel of St Mary's parish church at Limington, near Ilchester, founded in 1329 by Sir Richard de Gyvernay, has a high stone vault and five narrow bays with chamfered ribs. Further afield, the chantry chapel in the church at Willingham in Cambridgeshire has an acute-pointed angular-shaped stone roof over internal vaulting. In Scotland, Borthwick church and castle in Lothian, and many other buildings, also have solid stone roofs. The pierced arcaded parapet is reminiscent of a larger and unbuttressed fourteenth-century version on the Bishop's Palace at St David's in Wales.

The chapel's unusual features must have resulted from a deliberate architectural decision to fulfil a function. But what was this? The massive stone construction was surely intended to resist fire damage, or even damage from lightning, to which a conventional timber roof would have been susceptible. Attacks from French raiders along the south coast were regular occurrences in the 1330s during the wars with France, and the threat of fire was constant. Indeed, in 1336, because of the danger from French ships, vessels from Lyme Regis were instructed to assemble at Portsmouth to sail in convoy. In 1337, Edward III ordered warning beacons to be set up on the hilltops near Southampton, and in 1338, Melcombe Regis was given a grant to defend the town. Both Southampton and Portsmouth were attacked in 1338, and bonfires made of the towns.

The threat of invasion helps, too, to explain the extension of the north-west turret. With its advantageous prospect along the coast, it

probably served as a lookout to give warning of foreign ships and raiding parties; it was also used to alert local fishermen to shoals of fish, when a horn would be blown, as well as to eagerly awaited shipwrecks on the notorious Chesil Beach. Orc had been granted strand rights in the eleventh century; in 1289, the abbey's privilege of wreck was confirmed, and this included whales. Jealously guarded, the right was sometimes taken too far: in 1388, a shipowner complained that his cargo had been seized by the abbot and others, as though it had been a wreck.

The chapel became an important seamark and was therefore spared the fate of the monastery at the dissolution. Like many other churches, it was probably whitewashed to make it more visible.

The chapel's secular and ecclesiastical functions were all carried out, literally, over the heads of the abbey's tenants who ploughed, sowed, weeded and harvested the lynchet strips of the medieval fields on the hillside below (called St Katherine's Furlong in the sixteenth century). The Tor at Glastonbury has similar field lynchets, which would have been cultivated in the same way by the tenants of the abbot of Glastonbury. The contrast between the massive construction of the Abbotsbury chapel and the tenants' rude dwellings must have been very marked.

In 1742, a Mrs Horner is documented as having spent £50 on repairs to the chapel, and Lord Ilchester put the building in good state in about 1893. Further repairs were made in the 1960s and 70s, and in 1983 the entire roof was replaced with Clipsham stone. The chapel is now in the care of English Heritage.

# THE LEGEND OF ST CATHERINE OF ALEXANDRIA

CAROLINE TAYLOR

The chapel dedicated to St Catherine of Alexandria has stood on its hill above Abbotsbury for six hundred years, and we remember St Catherine in our 'catherine wheel' fireworks, but what of the saint herself?

To people in the Middle Ages, saints were thought of as intimate and trusted friends, involved in every aspect of life – and death – and, through their closeness to God, able to intercede on behalf of those on earth. St Catherine was one of the best loved of these saints, one of the 'Fourteen Holy Helpers' of German Catholicism. She was widely adopted as a patron saint and is represented in innumerable paintings, icons, sculptures, wall paintings and stained glass – often with the wheel and other symbols of her martyrdom. Artists painted her with loving affection and she is often seen in 'sacred conversation' with the Holy Family.

The dramatic story of St Catherine's martyrdom, true or not, was one to which a medieval audience would readily respond; her moral and physical courage in the face of tyrannical persecution and torture provided an edifying tale; and her subsequent role as the virgin 'bride' of Christ established her closeness to God.

14th-century mosaic icon of St Catherine, from the Baptistery of San Marco in Venice. Now in the V&A, London.

St Catherine (or Katharine; the original Greek form of her name, Ækaterina, means 'ever pure') is supposed to have died a martyr's death in Alexandria about AD 305. Descriptions of her passion exist from the ninth century, and some five hundred years after her death, in about 800, her bones were said to have been discovered on Mount Sinai. Relics of this kind were important both to the faithful and to the guardians of the shrine. The cult of St Catherine flourished, first at the Justinian monastery on Mount Sinai, which was renamed St Catherine's Monastery, and, over a century later, in the west, where it was enthusiastically adopted by Christians in Normandy and many other parts of Europe.

### ALEXANDRIA IN THE FIRST MILLENNIUM

The city in which St Catherine is supposed to have been born lies on the Mediterranean coast of North Africa, just west of the Nile delta. It was founded by Alexander the Great in 332 BC, and although essentially a Greek city, remained the capital of Egypt until AD 642, peopled by

Greeks, Africans, Jews, Romans – and, much later, Arabs. It was the chief seaport, from which grain for Jerusalem and Rome was exported, and became the cultural and intellectual hub of the Mediterranean, renowned not only for its great lighthouse (one of the seven wonders of the ancient world), its Mouseion (a centre of learning) and its palace, but also for the library which held over a million precious manuscripts. Mathematics, science, philosophy and theology flourished, with Jewish, Greek, pagan and, later, Christian scholars working together.

From 30 BC until AD 313 Alexandria was under the rule of Rome. By the second century the palace of Alexander's 'ideal' city was in ruins and the great library destroyed. Intellectual life, however, remained as vigorous as ever.

Christianity is said to have been introduced into Alexandria by St Mark as early as AD 45, but just as Egyptian and Greek deities had been amalgamated to form the Alexandrian god Serapis, so the early forms of Christian worship seem to have been confused with older practices. Christianity, like other religions, was tolerated by the Roman rulers, but when the worship of pagan gods faced serious threat from the rapidly increasing Christian and Jewish communities, persecution increased. Large numbers of Christians perished under Diocletian at the beginning of the fourth century, and the Egyptian Church (later to be named the

A 15th-century marble altarpiece, from the Capella di San Pietro in the Frari church, Venice. It shows St Catherine among the most venerated saints.

Stained glass showing the martyrdom of St Catherine, from the 13th-century church of St Mary at West Horsley, Surrey.

Coptic Church by the Arabs) dates its chronology from the 'Era of Martyrs' around AD 284.

Constantine I (312–37) finally established Christianity as the official religion of Rome, but Christians themselves were divided, partly on theological, partly on racial grounds. Alexandria remained the spiritual and intellectual capital of theological thought, but bitter disputes over the nature of God and Christ and the relationship of God to man led to schisms and hatred.

Although it was paganism not Christianity that symbolised learning and scientific thought in the early years of the first millennium, the first Christian institution of higher learning, the School of Alexandria, was founded in the mid second-century. Early Christian Platonist philosophers such as Pantaenus, Clement and Origen were attempting to establish orthodox Christian teaching, and to reconcile this with Greek culture, the ancient spiritual life of Egypt, and their own pagan upbringing. In this maelstrom of different cultures and creeds, religious differences often led to bloodshed.

During this period of persecution, Christians began to venerate the martyrs as saints, believing that those who suffered unto death for Christ were received directly into heaven and could thereby intercede for the living. The saints, in turn, were given the attributes of the pre-Christian deities, which helped the newly converted to make the transition from the old religion to the new.

## THE LEGEND OF ST CATHERINE

St Catherine of the legend was born of noble (or royal) pagan parents in third-century Alexandria. Beautiful and talented, she was well educated in languages, arts and science, and is said to have been converted to Christianity by a monk. The Roman emperor in Alexandria at the time was Maximinus, caesar of North Africa – one of the last of the pagan emperors before the Roman world became Christian under Constantine. When Maximinus ordered the Alexandrians to attend a ritual sacrifice, Catherine incited other Christians to refuse, and accused the emperor of persecution. The emperor called in fifty notable philosophers to argue the merits of paganism versus Christianity with her, but she converted them all and they were condemned to be burned alive. Seduced by her beauty, the emperor then offered her marriage; when she spurned him, he had her thrown into prison to starve, but a dove sent by God brought her food. The emperor's wife, intrigued, visited Catherine in prison and was converted, as were a centurion and two hundred soldiers who were later beheaded. Enraged, the emperor ordered that Catherine be tortured on revolving wheels armed with nails and knives; but the wheels shattered with such force that the knives spun off and killed many of the pagan spectators. In desperation, the emperor had her decapitated, and the wound flowed with milk instead of blood. Angels (or possibly monks, whose habit was described in Greek as 'angelic') then carried St Catherine's body to Mount Sinai on the rugged mountainous peninsula wedged between Africa and Asia, the site of Moses' encounter with God in the form of a burning bush.

The mystical marriage, from the entrance to St Catherine's Monastery, Mazzorbo, Venice.

This late 14th-century fresco from St Catherine's Convent in Treviso, in north-east Italy, was recently restored. It shows Christ between the Virgin Mary and St Catherine.

## THE CULT OF ST CATHERINE

In the ninth century, bones found on the Jebel Katharina in Sinai were claimed to be those of St Catherine. The relics were taken to the Greek Orthodox monastery founded by Justinian I in 527 on the slopes of Mount Sinai, and the monastery was renamed St Catherine's. The cult of St Catherine grew. In 1063, during the Crusades, a military order of St Catherine of Alexandria was founded (their insignia a sword within a spiked wheel), to guard the saint's relics and protect pilgrims to the monastery; returning crusaders, travelling monks and pilgrims helped to spread the legend abroad. Thanks to the relics of St Catherine at this remotest of all

Choir stalls from the Frari church, Venice, dated 1468.

Christian shrines, the monastery, dependent for its livelihood on pilgrimage, became in late medieval times the richest in Christendom. Today, pilgrims and tourists continue to visit St Catherine's Monastery for spiritual sustenance and to see its remarkable library, icons and mosaics.

In the early eleventh century, emissaries from Sinai are known to have been in Europe, spreading the cult of St Catherine and seeking funds for the monastery. In 1032, Simeon, a Sicilian monk from Sinai, carried some of the relics of St Catherine (her fingers) to Europe, He eventually deposited them in the (no longer extant) Benedictine monastery of Trinité-au-Mont above Rouen in Normandy. The monastery was renamed Ste Catherine-au-Mont, and her cult spread rapidly throughout Europe, especially, via Sicily, to Cyprus and Venice. The devotion to St Catherine assumed vast proportions after the Crusades, and received further support at the beginning of the fifteenth century when it was rumoured that she had appeared, with St Margaret (Queen of Scotland), to Joan of Arc.

It seems probable that St Catherine never existed, but to the people of the Middle Ages she was very real. She is listed in the Roman Martyrology, and martyrdoms have ever been the seed of the church for they lead to conversions. St Catherine quickly became one of the most venerated saints of the Christian calendar, both in the Roman Catholic church in the west and in Eastern Orthodoxy, where

A wooden statue of St Catherine in a church near Luzarches, north of Paris.

**S:CATHERINE**

many churches are dedicated to her. Her feast day, November 25th (or 24th), was celebrated in many parts of France with great solemnity and ceremonial as a holy day of obligation, and statues of St Catherine can still be found in many churches in France, Italy and Spain.

In England, St Catherine is especially associated with churches in Northamptonshire, Huntingdonshire, Cambridgeshire and the West Country. Sixty-two churches were dedicated to her, and 170 medieval church bells bear her name. The earliest known miracle play was written in her honour at Dunstable about 1110; wall paintings and stained glass tell the story of her life. Both Cambridge and Oxford Universities have colleges dedicated to her, and hospitals (alms houses –

*Early 14th-century stained glass figure of St Catherine from the Anglo-Saxon priory church at Deerhurst, Gloucestershire.*

lodgings for the elderly, the sick and for pilgrims) were founded
in her name. One, formerly at St Katharine's Dock below Tower
Bridge in London, moved later to Regents Park; another, in
Montpellier in France, was founded in the fifteenth century
for 'retired and repentent prostitutes'; at a hospital in
Bedminster, Bristol, founded by Robert de Berkeley in the
late twelfth century, secular priests wore a black or burnet
mantle with a St Catherine's wheel sewn on the left
breast. The hospital and chapel dedicated to St Catherine
in Dunfermline, Scotland, may have been built for
pilgrims visiting the shrine of St Margaret, while
Westminster Abbey's former Chapel of St Katherine
was the infirmary chapel for the monastery. Guilds
such as the Haberdashers' Company in London became
associated with her (usually through religious
confraternities formed to raise money for a shrine), and
until comparatively recent times there were any number
of 'Cat and Wheel' pubs, whose pub sign was a catherine
wheel. At Holt, in Wiltshire, 'cattern cakes' were sold on her
feast day until the late nineteenth century, and the church has catherine
wheels carved on the tower.

Medieval chapels dedicated to St Catherine were often built on cliffs or
hilltops. Dorset had hilltop chapels at Abbotsbury, Holworth, Milton
Abbas and Cerne Abbas, where the hill was known
as Cat and Chapel Hill. The clifftop chapel at Hartland
in Devon eventually fell into the sea. There were
chapels on St Catherine's Hill in Winchester and on
'Catelina Hill' near Christchurch in Hampshire, an
oratory on St Catherine Point in the Isle of Wight,
and others in France. Many of these Christian

places of worship lie on the site of earlier Saxon chapels or pre-Christian temples. St Augustine, instructing his priests who were setting out to convert the Anglo-Saxons at the end of the sixth century, wrote: 'I have decided after much thought about the English people, that their idol temples should not be destroyed, but only the idols themselves. Take holy water and sprinkle it on these shrines, build altars and place relics in them. For if the shrines are well built, it is essential that they should be converted from the worship of devils to the service of the true God. When this people see that their shrines are not destroyed they will be able to banish error from their hearts and be more ready to come to the places with which they are familiar, only now worshipping the name of the true God.'

St Catherine of Alexandria continues her appeal today. In Britain, convents, churches, windows (including that in the parish church of St Nicholas in Abbotsbury) have been dedicated to her even in the last hundred years.

Wessex probably became christianised in the middle of the seventh century, and as far as Abbotsbury is concerned, there is room for historical surmise. The chapel at Abbotsbury certainly sits on a typical temple platform, and St Catherine may perhaps have been a christianised version of a 'hidden' pagan moon goddess, with her wheel the sky. Christianised

The St Catherine window in St Nicholas's Church, Abbotsbury, by Anning Bell, 1910.

16

versions of pagan attributes certainly helped to make the new religion more accessible. In addition to this, the pagan goddess Astarte/Aphrodite, in her role as Queen of the Sky, was intimately connected with swans, and swans were almost certainly on the Fleet at Abbotsbury long before a monastery was founded there in the eleventh century.

In the early thirteenth century a version of the story of St Catherine was written in vernacular English; later in the century the legend was widely disseminated in western Europe by the *Legenda aurea*, a popularisation of edifying stories from monastic 'lectionaries', designed to give theological and moral guidance. The *Golden Legend* was soon translated into most European languages, and was one of the earliest printed books. Later versions of the stories include mention of St Catherine's 'mystical marriage' with Christ (though this was never a part of Eastern Orthodoxy), and paintings of this event abound from this time.

St Catherine is the patron saint of the Haberdashers' Company in the city of London. The painting comes from the company's earliest book of Ordinances, 1505.

St Catherine has always been associated with learning and abstract knowledge, and her independence and moral courage are qualities as relevant today as they ever were. She was an enemy to political extremism, religious oppression and tyranny, and used her remarkable gifts to lead the way for others to follow. She is also seen as a 'caring' saint: a defender of the underprivileged and the persecuted, and an adoring 'bride' to the infant (or occasionally adult) Christ.

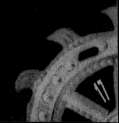

*The Virgin and Child with St John the Baptist and a Female Saint*, 1530–5, by Titian, showing St Catherine receiving a ring from the infant Christ. The painting is now in the National Gallery in London.

19

## THE MAKING OF SAINTS

Saints are venerated; God is adored. Sainthood is usually attributed to those whose real or alleged deeds and attributes continue to exert an influence after their death. A popular cult or folk belief may, however, attribute saintly qualities to a person long before institutional religion confirms it. St Catherine was popularly acclaimed in this way.

Canonisation in the Roman Catholic church leads to the inclusion of the saintly candidate in the canon of saints and full public veneration. It requires, among other things, evidence of a reputation for sanctity or heroic virtue and proof that the candidate had wrought miracles during his or her lifetime. A step on the way to canonisation is 'beatification'. In Eastern Orthodoxy, the process of canonisation results in a solemn proclamation and is based on the spontaneous devotion towards an individual by the faithful.

A wooden statue of St Catherine, part of a Renaissance altarpiece from Lugo cathedral in north-west Spain. Lugo was on the pilgrim route (the *Camino Francés*) from France to Santiago de Compostela.

Saints in the Roman Catholic church are seen as representatives of God's grace on earth, and are venerated as moral examples and as mediators capable of interceding between the faithful and God; the expression 'dear saints' indicates an emotional tie. In Eastern Orthodoxy they are seen as teachers and friends, ambassadors to God, who pray with the faithful and assist in their spiritual ascent.

Saints provided an essential link between pre-Christian religious practices and Christianity. Saints were often endowed with the same attributes as the pagan gods and goddesses, making the new religion appear less strange. And their relics (soon deliberately spread throughout Christendom) gave tangible evidence of their efficacy as holy healers.

## ST CATHERINE AS PATRON SAINT

St Catherine became the patron saint of wheelwrights and any whose work involved wheels (such as engineers, spinners, potters and millers); of unmarried young women (either because she spurned the emperor's advances or because she became the virgin 'bride of Christ'); of philosophers and men of learning (because of her persuasive logic); of students and teachers (because of her learning: she was the patron saint of Paris University, where diplomas, awarded on November 25th, were called *'catherinettes'*; and also of Oxbridge colleges); of wet nurses (because she bled milk, not blood); of the caring professions: nurses and doctors; of the sick and dying; of the underprivileged: prostitutes, servants; and in the seventeenth century she was also adopted by weavers in Somerset and pipe makers in Rouen, who stamped the bowls of their clay pipes with a catherine wheel.

The delightful but heart-rending prayer in St Catherine's Chapel at Abbotsbury is to the patron saint of the unmarried:

*A husband, St Catherine,*
*A handsome one, St Catherine,*
*A rich one, St Catherine,*
*A nice one, St Catherine,*
*And soon, St Catherine.*

A very similar one is found at a shrine to St Catherine by a pool at Lyons-la-Forêt in Normandy (*De pitié, donnez nous un époux / Car nous brûlons d'aimer* ...). In Italy and France, unmarried young women of twenty-five, *catherinettes*, were given the privilege of adorning statues of St Catherine in the churches for the

Pen-and-ink drawing of St Catherine, dated 1573, by Hans Sebald Beham, from Chatsworth, Derbyshire

saint's feast day. Even today the expressions *'elle coiffe Ste Catherine'* and 'she braids St Catherine's tresses' are used of young women who appear unlikely to get married. *Catherinette* parties are still held in France, as something of a joke, on November 25th, when the *haute couture* trade in Paris dresses its models in extravagent hats in the colours of St Catherine – yellow (for the passage of time) and green (for hope). And young women still visit St Catherine's Chapel in Abbotsbury to wish for a husband.

## RELICS AND PILGRIMAGES IN MEDIEVAL CHRISTIANITY

The veneration of the relics of a saint began in the first centuries of Christianity, and popes later approved the dispersal of relics in order to strengthen the faith of newly converted communities. Pilgrims in the Middle Ages would travel, sometimes enormous distances and in extremes of danger and discomfort, to worship at a saint's shrine, in the belief that through the intercession of the saint their prayers and wishes would be heard by God, their sins would be forgiven, and that the labour of their journey would earn 'indulgence' from the time spent in purgatory, hovering over the fiery pit of hell. A pilgrimage to the shrine of St Catherine, the farthest away of all the

A late 15th-century English stone statuette of St Catherine, with the wheel and sword of her martyrdom, trampling the Emperor Maximinus underfoot. At 86 cm, it is taller than many similar statuettes. Now in the Musée des Antiquités in Rouen.

Christian shrines, would earn rich spiritual rewards for the pilgrim – as well as bringing wealth to the monastery. In Eastern Orthodoxy such veneration was often directed to icons.

People also believed that the saint's mortal remains, or objects that had been in contact with the saint, could work miracles. The bones of the saint would often be described as exuding a holy oil which had the power to protect and to heal. The first Christian reference to relics describes handkerchiefs carried from the body of St Paul to heal the sick. Later, bread was rubbed on the bones of a saint and taken home to feed to those who were ill. At Liberton, on the outskirts of Edinburgh, there is a balm well, St Katherine's Well. The oily spring is said to have issued from the ground where a drop of oil from St Catherine's bones fell on its way from Sinai to Queen Margaret (St Margaret) of Scotland. In 1504, James IV made an offering to 'Sanct Katrine's of the oly well'. The *Golden Legend* describes oil issuing continuously from St Catherine's bones, which had the power to mend all physical ailments.

A lead pilgrim's badge from Rouen in Normandy. These badges were usually pierced so that they could be attached to clothing, but sometimes had pins on the back.

Once, when a pilgrim was visiting the shrine of St Catherine on Sinai to collect some of the holy oil, the saint's fingers apparently snapped off. It was this precious relic that the monk Simeon took with him on his journey to Europe.

'Reliquary' churches not only made the relics available to the faithful; they also brought credibility and wealth to the foundation. Indulgences could be sold, and, as today, souvenirs, food and lodging brought

23

in money. In the later Middle Ages, chapels and churches, or simply altars dedicated to the cult of a saint were built, and confraternities established, to raise money for a distant shrine. However, abuses of the system (the sale of indulgences; the rooking of pilgrims by the unscrupulous; increasing doubt about the value of pilgrimages as a way to salvation) helped to pave the way to the Reformation.

Pilgrimages were remarkably well organised. First, permission had to be gained from the local priest, or safe conducts acquired for pilgrims going to the Holy Land. Arrangements were made for the safekeeping of the pilgrim's land, possessions and family while he was away (sometimes for years). Money could be deposited at centres along the route, but the poor would rely on alms and on lodging in hospitals along the way. Guides and itineraries were available, and travelling emissaries from the shrines could provide advice. Pilgrims usually wore the same 'uniform': a heavy cloak, a broad-brimmed hat (often adorned with badges from the shrines visited), a wooden staff with a water-carrier tied to it, and a satchel or 'scrip'. Pilgrims would return, much as today, with souvenirs of their pilgrimage: badges or medallions (usually made of lead or tin alloy) of their chosen saint or his or her symbols.

Two 15th-century lead pilgrim's badges. The one on the left was found while dragging the Seine in Paris and is now in the Musée des Antiquités in Rouen, Normandy. The one above was found in the Thames in London and is now in the British Museum, London.

## CHRISTENDOM IN THE MIDDLE AGES

After the collapse of the social and political structures of the vast Roman Empire in AD 410, 'Christendom' provided the only cohesive order in an increasingly chaotic Europe. Apart from a brief period of political and cultural stability under Charlemagne, the church in Rome came to dominate political, intellectual and cultural life.

St Catherine's mystical
marriage, by a
Venetian painter,
c. 1500, in the Sacristy
of the Frari church,
Venice.

Gradually, Europe became, if not more stable, at least more ordered. The tentacles of papal power reached to its furthest corners, but an increase in artistic and commercial secular activity independent of the church slowly began to emerge. Other social and political organisations followed, and the thirteenth century saw the apex of medieval civilisation in the west.

St Catherine's mystical marriage, by a Venetian painter, c. 1500, in the Sacristy of the Frari church, Venice.

## THE SYMBOLISM OF CHRISTIAN ICONOGRAPHY

Until the late Middle Ages, most art (with many notable Saxon exceptions in England) was religious in inspiration. In the west, paintings, stained glass, wallpaintings, mosaics, carvings in wood, alabaster, stone and ivory, statuettes made of pipeclay were used to inspire the faithful.

The symbolism of this iconography would have been readily understood by a still mainly illiterate society. In representations of St Catherine, for example, the wheel represents her torture; a sword or palm, her martyrdom; a book, learning and wisdom; a crown, her royal origins (her clothes in the icons of Eastern Orthodoxy are those of the imperial court, indicating royal blood); and the ring in Catholic iconography represents her mystical marriage to Christ. She is also sometimes seen grinding the Emperor Maximinus underfoot. The commonest clues to St Catherine are the wheel and the mystic marriage.

Statue of St Catherine crushing the emperor Maximus, outside the church of La Santa Pastora, Burgos, Spain.

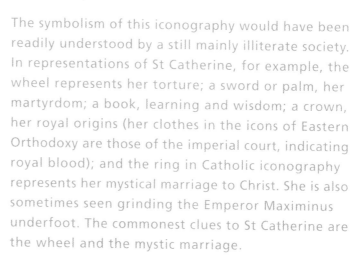

## SAINTS AND THE REFORMATION

The twelfth and thirteenth centuries saw a tremendous religious revival in England and throughout Europe, of which the cult of saints was an integral part, although the cult of St Catherine seems to have reached its height in Roman Catholic Europe in the sixteenth and seventeenth centuries. In Dorset alone, chantries were dedicated to St Catherine in churches at Marnhull, Shaftesbury Abbey, Sherborne Abbey and Gillingham.

However, the Reformation in the mid sixteenth century brought a dramatic change in the role of saints in Protestant worship. The colourful paraphernalia of the medieval church was swept away, along with its many abuses, in favour of direct communication with God through prayer, faith and religious conscience. The importance of visual images in stimulating religious

15th-century grisaille wallpainting of St Catherine, from Eton College Chapel, Windsor.

A nearly life-size wooden statue of St Catherine from the Cistercian monastery of Las Huelgas in Burgos, northern Spain.

A life-size wooden statue of St Catherine from the medieval cathedral of Santiago de Compostela in north-west Spain, one of the major centres of pilgrimage in the Middle Ages.

('idolatrous') fervour gave way to the Word, leaving little room for the saints who, if they were retained, lost their intercessionary powers and were demoted to mere moral examples. After 1530, the feast day of St Catherine (along with those of many other saints) no longer appears as a holy day in *The Book of Common Prayer*, although her feast day is listed in the Calendar of the 1614 edition.

There are virtually no statues of St Catherine left in this country (though there are plenty in the churches of Italy, Spain and France); wall paintings were painted or panelled over; while expensive stained glass was often left but had the saint's face blanked out. It may have been necessary reform, but rather drove the 'merrie' out of King Hal's England.

## THE DECLINE OF ST CATHERINE

In the latter part of the seventeenth century, the French religious writer and orator J.-B. Bossuet, bishop of Meaux and religious adviser to Louis XIV, wrote a number of panegyrics, one of the most beautiful of which was to St Catherine. However, doubt had been cast on the authenticity of St Catherine's life, and by the end of the eighteenth century her feast day had been removed from the Catholic Breviary in Paris. She continued to be an inspiration to artists, and no doubt to the faithful, but was gradually pushed to the margin of mainstream Catholicism. She was finally removed from the Universal Calendar of Saints in 1969, on the grounds that 'she probably never existed', but is still revered in Eastern Orthodoxy as one of the two most important saints, with St Irene.

**Stained glass of c. 1290 in the Chapter House vestibule of York Minster shows St Catherine. Glass elsewhere in the church illustrates scenes from her life.**

It is possible that St Catherine was simply an invention of the monastery on Mount Sinai. E.M. Forster, in his evocative *Alexandria – a history and guide*, says dismissively of St Catherine: 'She and her wheel were creations of western Catholicism, and the land of her supposed suffering has only recognised her out of politeness to the French.' What seems probable is that her story was confused with that of a remarkable pagan woman philosopher and mathematician, Hypatia, who is known to have lived in Alexandria later in the fourth century and was barbarously done to death with tiles by fanatical Christians. She is said to have had many of the same attributes (intellect, beauty, steadfastness in the face of torture). Forster, on the other hand, describes her as 'a middle-aged lady who taught mathematics in the Mouseion'. Whatever the truth of it, St Catherine represents for us, as she did for medieval believers, a model of intellectual and moral courage; a model of trust in God; and a guide in a world of continuing religious and political intolerance.

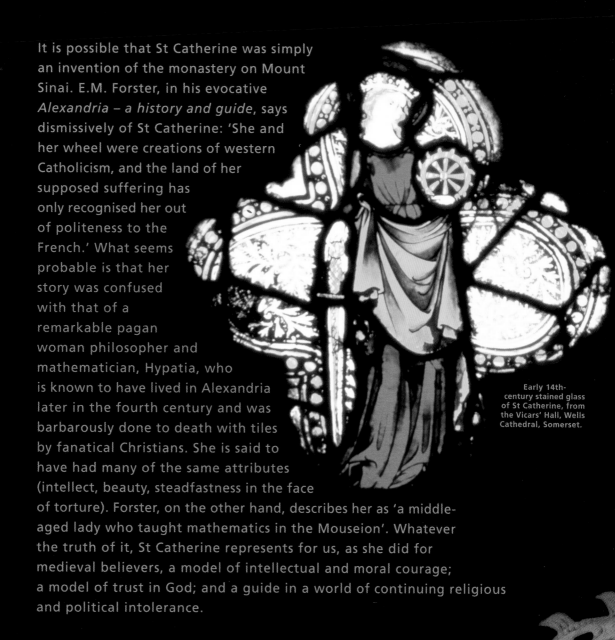

Early 14th-century stained glass of St Catherine, from the Vicars' Hall, Wells Cathedral, Somerset.

## ST CATHERINE TODAY

The pursuit of St Catherine in Europe today has proved a fascinating task; even in Britain where so much iconographic material was destroyed at the dissolution of the monasteries, during the Reformation and under Cromwell, much remains or has been rediscovered: marvellous stained-glass cycles or individual figures of St Catherine in cathedrals and churches from Yorkshire to Cornwall; chapels named after her in country places or as part of great cathedrals; carved bench ends like those at Combeinteignhead in Devon or Beverley in Yorkshire; wall paintings like those found behind panelling in Eton College chapel, or plastered over at St Kyneburgha in Castor, Cambridgeshire and St Swithin's in Old Weston, Huntingdonshire; a headless stone sculpture of St Catherine with her wheel, discovered in the grounds of the former Cistercian monastery of Forde abbey in Dorset; or charming pilgrims' badges, pipeclay statuettes, rings and seals dug out of river mud on the foreshore of the Thames and the Seine, and now in the Museum of London, the British Museum and museums in Normandy. Oxbridge colleges have marvellous silver engraved with catherine wheels, and the Haberdashers' Company in London even has a figurehead of St Catherine that used to adorn a barge on the Thames. And many, many visitors continue to be drawn to the little chapel on the hill above Abbotsbury.

Taken from a postcard provided by St Catherine's College, Cambridge.

A wooden bench end from the (restored) 14th-/15th-century church at Combeinteignhead, Devon.

A 13th- or 14th-century stone statue of St Catherine, which was found, together with one of St Margaret, at Forde Abbey in Dorset, a former Cistercian monastery. St Catherine and St Margaret were immensely popular saints and are often found side by side.

## THE MONASTERY OF
## ST CATHERINE ON MOUNT SINAI

The Greek Orthodox monastery on Mount Sinai is the oldest monastery in the world. This is the place where Moses, in the Wilderness, spoke to God through the Burning Bush; on the summit of Mount Sinai, God handed Moses the Tablets of Stone.

Justinian's fortified monastery with its great basilica was built in the sixth century to serve both sacred and secular purposes. It gathered and protected scattered monastic communities, allowing them to continue a life of spiritual asceticism undisturbed. It also maintained close relations and shared  mutual respect with the bedouin, even after their conversion to the Muslim faith following the Arab conquest of AD 641. In the eleventh century a mosque was built inside the monastery walls. As a result, the monastery was able to exert a profound influence on the entire area.

The discovery of St Catherine's relics in the ninth century, and their removal to the Sinai monastery, began to attract pilgrims. Her cult spread throughout Europe from the eleventh century, leading to streams of pilgrims and travellers to her shrine in the next centuries. The monastery became the richest in Christendom.

Isolated from Byzantium, the monastery's treasures avoided destruction during a century of iconoclasm in the eighth and ninth centuries. Conserved with loving care are icons from the sixth, seventh and eighth centuries; codices and scrolls dating from the fourth century; beautiful manuscripts copied at the monastery from the tenth century. The monastery remains a spiritual stronghold and, as ever, a place of pilgrimage, continuing to welcome worshippers, pilgrims and tourists of all nationalities and all faiths.

In 1996, the St Catherine Foundation was inaugurated in London (with HRH the Prince of Wales, the Church of England Archbishop of Canterbury, the Roman Catholic Archbishop of Westminster and the Greek Orthodox Archbishop of Thyateria and Great Britain as four of the trustees) to help support the work of the great library at the St Catherine Monastery.

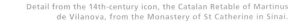
Detail from the 14th-century icon, the Catalan Retable of Martinus de Vilanova, from the Monastery of St Catherine in Sinai.

## JOHN DRYDEN AND THE ABBOTSBURY MUSIC FESTIVAL

Dryden (1631–1700) wrote a play, published in 1670, ten years after the Restoration of Charles II, entitled *Tyrannick Love*. Based on the life of St Catherine, who is seen as a 'loyall martyr', the play uses the basic conflict between Christian and pagan to reflect the religious conflict in post-Cromwellian Britain. It was intended as a compliment to Protestant King Charles's Catholic Queen, Catherine of Braganza.

The English public at that time enjoyed plays relating to political and social life, and tyrants (Charles I; Cromwell himself; the outrageous Maxim of the play) were of popular concern. Dryden wrote several plays on the theme of tyrants. After the first performance of *Tyrannick Love*, Nell Gwynne spoke a rather silly epilogue which had such an effect that Charles II immediately rushed backstage.

A play about St Catherine had obvious relevance to Abbotsbury and its chapel, and Dryden's play has political relevance to many parts of the world today. To celebrate the Millennium, Abbotsbury Music decided to commission music from a British composer, Ronan Magill (who studied under Benjamin Britten), to accompany a shortened version of *Tyrannick Love*. The play itself was adapted by Peter and Barbara Laurie and the production directed by Nell Coleman. This book had its origins as part of the Millennium project.

And the chapel remains.

## ILLUSTRATIONS

FRONT COVER LEFT AND TITLE PAGE: 15th-century stained glass of St Catherine by Peter Hemmel von Andlau, from Kloster Nonnberg in Salzburg, Austria
– © Sonia Halliday & Laura Lushington.
FRONT COVER RIGHT: St Catherine's Chapel, Abbotsbury. Seen from the north-west, the chapel looks out over Lyme Bay and Portland can be seen beyond
– © Michael J Allen.
BACK COVER, LEFT: English 15th-century alabaster relief of St Catherine, 43cm high, from the Musée d'Evreux in Normandy. Crowned, she carries the wheel on which she was tortured and the sword with which she was decapitated. Traces of the original polychrome colouring have been carefully restored
– © Collection Musée d'Evreux, photo Jean-Pierre Godais.
BACK COVER, CENTRE: the chapel at Abbotsbury seen from the south-east – © Francesca Radcliffe.
BACK COVER, RIGHT: 14th-/15th-century wooden bench end from Combeinteignhead Church, Devon
– © Francesca Radcliffe.
PAGE: 1 – © West Dorset Tourism.
PAGES: 2, 3 bottom, 4, 5, 33 – © Peter Laurie.
PAGES: 3 top & middle, 6, 9, 11 left, 12 right, 13, 16, 20, 25, 27, 28, 30 left & bottom right, 34
– © Francesca Radcliffe.
PAGE: 8 – © V&A Picture Library, London.
PAGE: 10 – NMR © B T Batsford Ltd.
PAGES: 11 right, 22, 24 left – © Musées départementaux de la Seine Maritime, photos Yohann Deslandes.
PAGE: 12 bottom left – © Museo Civico, Treviso.
PAGE: 14 – © Deerhurst Priory Church.
PAGE: 15 top – © Museum of London.
PAGES: 15 bottom, 17 – © Haberdashers' Company.
PAGES: 18, 19 – © National Gallery, London.
PAGE: 21 – © the Duke of Devonshire and the Chatsworth Settlement Trustees.
PAGES: 23, 24 right – © British Museum, London.
PAGE: 26 – © Eton College, photo Mark Phillips.
PAGE: 29 – © Dean and Chapter of Wells Cathedral, photo Richard Neale.
PAGE: 30 top right – © St Catharine's College, Cambridge.
PAGES: 31, 32 – © St Catherine Foundation, Sinai.

## ACKNOWLEDGEMENTS

I should like to thank the following for their kindness and patience in providing information, illustrations, answers to questions, and stimulating comments: Barbara and Peter Laurie and Francesca Radcliffe of Abbotsbury Music for much initial research, help, encouragement and photography; Laurence Keen, former Dorset County Archaeologist; Dr Robert Dunning, editor of the Victoria History of Somerset; Deacon Oakes of the Archdiocese of Thyateira and Great Britain; Derek Hall, Suat Ltd; the St Catherine Foundation; John Cope, the Haberdashers' Company; Professor J.H. Baker, St Catharine's College, Cambridge; Dr John Jones, Balliol College, Oxford; Professor Peter Rickard, Emmanuel College, Cambridge; the Society of Antiquaries; St Andrews University Library; English Heritage's NMR; John Clark, the Museum of London; Lisa Voden-Decker, the British Museum; Sophie Demoy, Musée des Antiquités, Rouen; Sabina de Minerbi; Elizabeth Fortescue; the Revd C.W. Mitchell-Innes, Conduct of Eton College; HRH the Prince of Wales for introducing me to the St Catherine Foundation's The Monastery of St Catherine; any number of friends and relations who have pointed me in useful directions and checked the text; and last, but not least, Peter Yeoman, County Archaeologist for Fife, whose book, Pilgrimage in Medieval Scotland, brought the whole business of saints, relics and pilgrimages to life.     Caroline Taylor

Abbotsbury Music would like to thank the Arts Council of England, Southwest Arts, the Millennium Lottery Fund, the D'Oyly Carte Charitable Trust, West Dorset District Council, English Heritage, Martin and Francesca Radcliffe, and the Haberdashers' Company, for generous financial support for their Millennium project.

A 15th-century stained glass window in the Frari church, Venice, showing St Catherine.

34